The INCAS

Revised and Updated

JANE SHUTER

Heinemann Library
Chicago, Illinois

©2002, 2009 Heinemann Library
a division of Pearson Inc.
Chicago, Illinois

Customer Service 888-454-2279
Visit our website at www.heinemannraintree.com

Photo research by Mica Brancic
Designed by Richard Parker and Manhattan Design
Printed and bound in China by CTPS

13 12 11 10 09
10 9 8 7 6 5 4 3 2 1

New edition ISBNs: 978-1-4329-1329-8 (hardcover)
                       978-1-4329-1337-3 (paperback)

J 985.019 Shuter

The Library of Congress has cataloged the first edition as follows:
Shuter, Jane
The Incas / Jane Shuter
p. cm. – (History opens windows)
Includes bibliographic references and index.
Summary: Presents an overview of the Incan culture, examining such topics as government, religion, domestic life, recreation, occupations, entertainment, food, shelter, and clothing.
ISBN 978-1-58810-590-5 (1-58810-590-3) (HC)
ISBN 978-1-4034-0025-3 (1-4034-0025-3) (Pbk)
Incas – History – Juvenile Literature. 2. Incas – Social Life and customs – Juvenile Literature. [1. Incas. 2. Indians of South America.] I. Title. II. Series.
F3429 .S546 2002
985. 01 – dc21

                              2001004027

Acknowledgments
The author and publishers are grateful to the following for permission to reproduce photographs: p. 6 © Neg. no 5068(2), photo by John Bigelow Taylor, courtesy of the Library, American Museum of Natural History; pp. 7, 18 © Gianni Dagli Orti/Corbis; p. 9 © Art Resource; p. 10 © Bridgeman Art Library/Museo Arqueologia, Lima, Peru; p. 12, © Getty Images/Digital Vision; p. 13 © Nathan Benn/Corbis; p. 14 © The Art Archive; pp. 15, 23 © Werner Forman/Art Resource; p. 16 © The Pitt Rivers Museum, University of Oxford; p. 17 © John Bigelow Taylor/Art Resource; p. 19 © Neg. no 5087(3), photo by John Bigelow Taylor, courtesy of the Library, American Museum of Natural History; p. 20 © Getty Images/Stone/Robert Frerck; p. 21 © Roman Soumar/Corbis; p. 22 © Tony Morrison/South American Pictures; p. 24 © The British Museum; p. 25 © Neg. no 5094(3), photo by John Bigelow Taylor, courtesy of the Library, American Museum of Natural History; p. 26 © Neg. no 5070(2), photo by John Bigelow Taylor, courtesy of the Library, American Museum of Natural History; p. 28 © Neg. no 5088(2), photo by John Bigelow Taylor, courtesy of the Library, American Museum of Natural History; p. 30 © Charles and Josette Lenars/Corbis.

Illustrations: p. 4 Eileen Mueller Neill; pp. 8, 11, 27, 29 James Mitchell.
Cover photograph courtesy of © Masterfile.

Every effort has been made to contact copyright holders of any material reproduced in this book. Any omissions will be rectified in subsequent printings if notice is given to the publisher.

Disclaimer
All the Internet addresses (URLs) given in this book were valid at the time of going to press. However, due to the dynamic nature of the Internet, some addresses may have changed, or sites may have changed or ceased to exist since publication. While the author and publisher regret any inconvenience this may cause readers, no responsibility for any such changes can be accepted by either the author or the publisher.

Contents

Some words are shown in bold, **like this**.
You can find out what they mean by looking in the glossary.

Introduction

This map shows the Inca empire at its biggest, in about 1520.

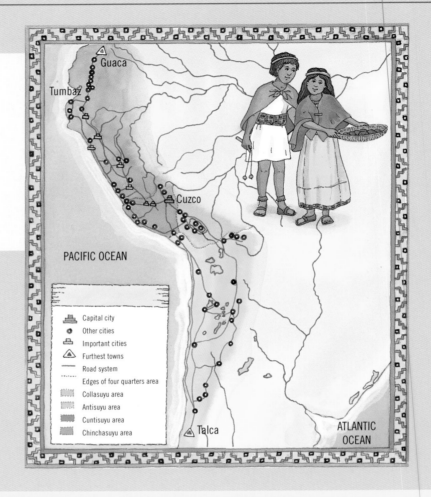

Guaca

Tumbaz

Cuzco

PACIFIC OCEAN

Capital city
Other cities
Important cities
Furthest towns
Road system
Edges of four quarters area
Collasuyu area
Antisuyu area
Cuntisuyu area
Chinchasuyu area

Talca

ATLANTIC OCEAN

1200	1300
Incas wandering	Early period

Inca first settle
at Cuzco

The Incas were a group of wandering people who settled in modern Peru in about 1200. They built a city called Cuzco and farmed the land around it. Sometimes the Incas got along well with nearby groups of people and traded with them. At other times they fought these groups, and sometimes they raided them to take things they needed. This often happened in times when food ran short.

Then, in 1438, Pachacuti became the *Sapa Inca*, or ruler, of the Incas. Almost at once he began to build an **empire**. He did this by taking over other lands, either by force or by making an agreement with the people who lived there. In less than 100 years, the empire expanded to cover most of modern Peru and parts of modern Chile, Argentina, and Bolivia.

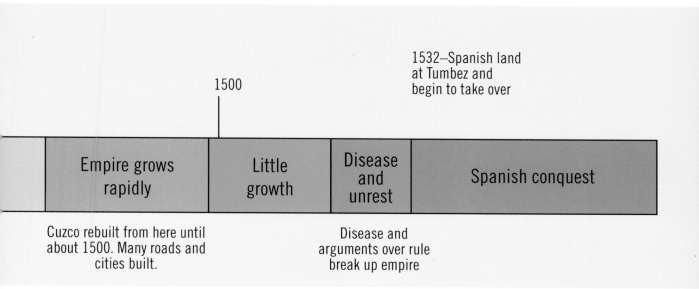

1532—Spanish land at Tumbez and begin to take over

1500

| Empire grows rapidly | Little growth | Disease and unrest | Spanish conquest |

Cuzco rebuilt from here until about 1500. Many roads and cities built.

Disease and arguments over rule break up empire

How Were the Incas Ruled?

The Incas were ruled by a single person, the *Sapa Inca*. He owned all the land and made all the laws. Unless he died suddenly, each *Sapa Inca* chose who would rule after him. He and the next ruler ruled together for a while so there was no sudden change.

Each *Sapa Inca* ruled from the city of Cuzco, no matter how big the Inca **empire** grew. Each of them built a new palace in the city and set up a new royal *ayllu*, or family. The old royal *ayllu* continued to live in the old palace.

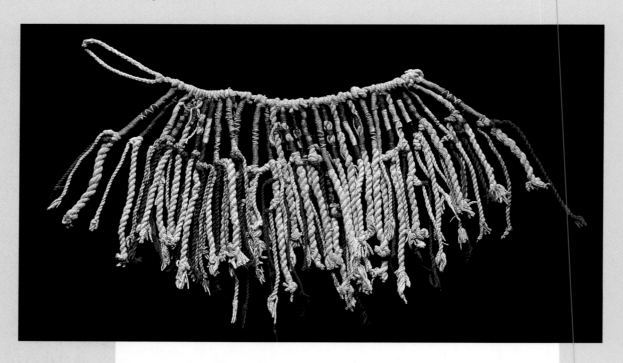

The Incas had no written language. People memorized messages to pass them on. Some lists were kept by knotting different colored strings with different types of knots. These are called *quipu*.

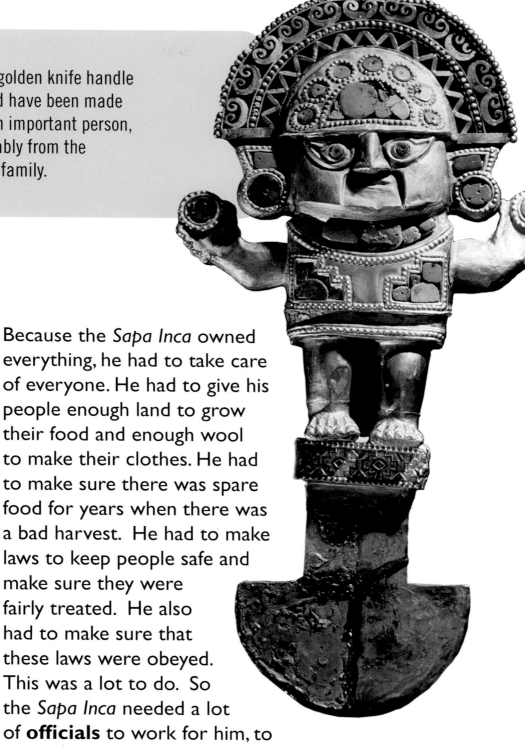

This golden knife handle would have been made for an important person, probably from the royal family.

Because the *Sapa Inca* owned everything, he had to take care of everyone. He had to give his people enough land to grow their food and enough wool to make their clothes. He had to make sure there was spare food for years when there was a bad harvest. He had to make laws to keep people safe and make sure they were fairly treated. He also had to make sure that these laws were obeyed. This was a lot to do. So the *Sapa Inca* needed a lot of **officials** to work for him, to make sure everything got done.

Building an Empire

The different colors on this map show how the Inca empire grew.

Inca-controlled land by 1471
Inca-controlled land by 1493
Inca-controlled land by 1525
City and center of other group taken over by Incas

• Chimu

Moche • • Chan Chan

Chancay

Paracas • • Cuzco
Nozca

Pacific Ocean

N
O
E
W
S

The Inca **empire** grew very quickly after 1438. The Incas would go to the ruler of an area and ask him to join the Inca empire. If he said no, the Inca army went in and took the land by force. The defeated leader had to come and live in Cuzco. He was allowed to live like a **noble**, but he was really a prisoner. This way the Incas could be sure that his people accepted the Inca rule.

Once the Incas took over an area, they made the people learn *Quechua*, the Inca language. They made them obey Inca laws and worship the Inca Sun god. If they had taken over by force, they sometimes moved the local people to different parts of the empire, to make a rebellion (uprising against a ruler or government) less likely. *Mitimaes* moved into the new land. These were settlers loyal to the Incas.

There were good things about Inca rulers. They built good roads, as well as cities and public water supplies. They saw that everyone had food, clothes, and a place to live.

People in conquered lands brought new skills and styles of crafts to the Inca empire. These beakers are made in the *Chimu* style.

Running an Empire

The Incas called their **empire** Tahuantinsuyu. This means "land of the four quarters." The *Sapa Inca*, who ruled from Cuzco, had many **officials**. They carried out his laws, collected his taxes, and made sure all **duty work** was done. (Duty work was done by everyone who was not a noble as a kind of tax.) An important Inca **noble** ran each of the four quarters of the empire. Each of them had several less important governors to run parts of each quarter. They could be Incas or lords from groups the Incas had taken over.

Under the governors came several levels of officials called *curacas*. The most important of these reported to the governor and controlled groups of up to 10,000 households. The least important controlled groups of only 10 households.

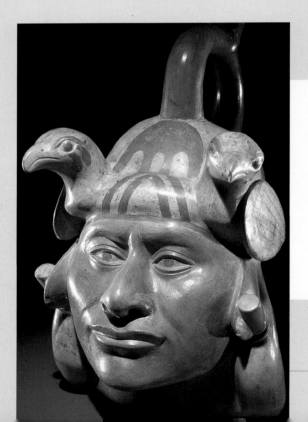

This pottery head represents a warrior. The Inca army kept control of the empire, so warriors were important people.

Sapa Inca

Four Inca governors—
one for each quarter

Local governors for large areas

Important *curacas* ran groups
of 1,000-10,000 households

Less important *curacas* ran groups
of about 100 households

The least important *curacas*
controlled 10 heads of household

Roads and Transportation

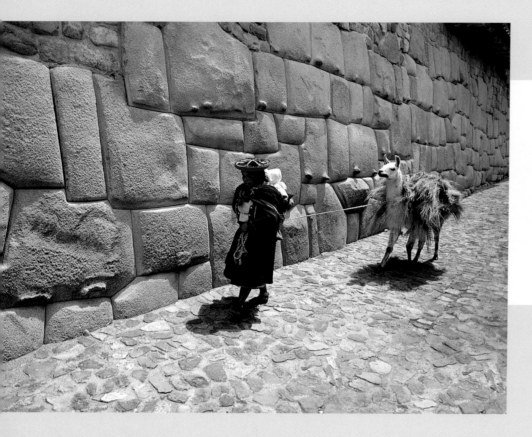

This street in Cuzco, Peru, still has the original Inca road surface and walls.

The Incas did not have wheeled carts or wagons. Instead, people walked or traveled by canoe. Important people were often carried in chairs on poles when they traveled a long distance. Llamas were used to carry loads. The Incas needed to be able to move around the **empire** easily. They built a road system that covered about 14,000 miles (22,500 km) and linked almost all the main towns. The roads were up to 33 feet (10 meters) wide near big towns. In the mountains they could be as little as 3 feet (1 meter) wide. They had steps, tunnels, and bridges in the mountains.

Not many traders or ordinary people used the Inca roads. They were mostly used to keep the empire running. Government **officials** traveled on them to carry out inspections. The army used the roads to travel quickly.

Tambos lined the main roads. These were places for officials to rest or stay in when visiting nearby villages. The Incas also built storehouses near the roads. Officials sent messages along the roads using trained runners, or *chasquis*. These runners passed along either **quipu** or spoken messages. A message could be sent to someone about 150 miles (240 km) away in just one day.

These ear ornaments show Inca runners. They are shown with wings because the runners were so fast!

Trade and Crafts

The Incas did not trade much outside the **empire**.
Villages tried to grow and make everything they needed.
Trade was controlled by the government, which made
rules about trading at markets. There were craft
workers who made beautiful things, but these were
mostly for the *Sapa Inca* and his **nobles**. Craft workers
could give the things they made instead of doing
duty work.

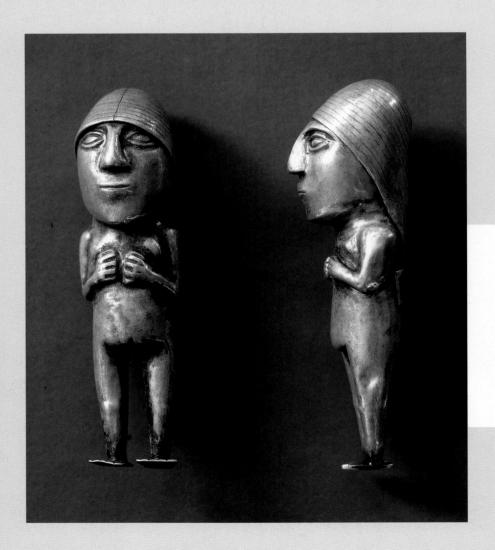

Skilled craft
workers made
this silver model
of a woman.

Most craft workers lived and worked in the towns and cities. Those who were the most skilled had workshops in the royal palace. They made things for the *Sapa Inca* and his family. Different parts of the empire were known for people who were skilled in different crafts. The Moche people, for example, produced beautiful pottery, often in the shapes of people or animals. The Paracas people were especially good weavers.

This carved wooden beaker was used during religious **ceremonies**. It shows the head of a noble.

Weaving

This weaving basket is more than 500 years old. The vegetable dyes used on the yarn still have not faded.

Weaving was one of the most important Inca crafts. The *Sapa Inca* often gave pieces of cloth as presents to **nobles** or to the important people from other groups that were part of the **empire**. Inca women spun their thread so finely and wove it so tightly that the cloth was very good at keeping out the cold. Cloth for a shirt, made on a modern weaving machine, has about 60 **weft** threads in each inch. Ordinary Inca weavers made cloth with 200 weft threads to the inch. The best weavers could fit 500 weft threads into an inch.

The government divided weavers into four groups. There were rules about the kinds of cloth each group could make, and about the colors and decoration they could use.

The first groups were ordinary people who wove their own cloth at home. Weaving was not their only job. The other three groups were all full-time weavers. The *Hatan Runa* did the most basic weaving, such as ordinary clothes. The *Cumbi Camayoc* were more skillful and wove cloth for the nobles and for the *Sapa Inca* to give as presents. The most important weavers were the *Mamacuna*, who wove cloth for the **temples** and for the *Sapa Inca*.

This woven **tunic** has many colors and complicated patterns. It required skillful weaving and was probably made for a noble.

Cities

Inca buildings in the cities were made of stone and had high walls with no windows. The streets were paved and narrow. Government **officials** ran the **empire** from these cities, and priests held religious **ceremonies** at the **temples**. The *Sapa Inca* and his family lived in a palace in Cuzco. Behind the palace was a school where the boys who would one day run the empire were taught how to make and read *quipu*. They also learned math, astronomy, history, and mapmaking. The homes and workshops of various craft workers were farther from the city.

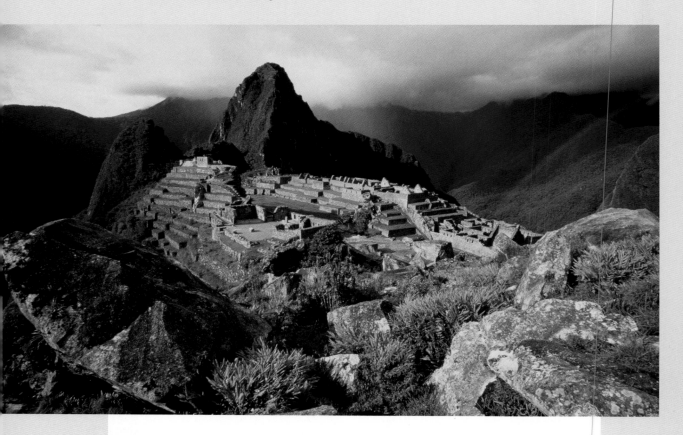

The city of Machu Picchu was built on a mountaintop, very close to an even higher mountain. Its location may have given it special religious importance.

You can see how well the stones in this Inca wall fit together and how they curve in where they join.

Cities were built from stone. The blocks were of different colors and sizes, depending on how important the building was. Buildings were not decorated with carvings on the outside. Instead, the stones were carefully smoothed and often curved in to the point where they joined.

Inca builders did not use any **mortar** to fix the stones together. The stones were carved so exactly to shape that they fitted perfectly. This method of building meant that in earthquakes, which happened often, the blocks of stone "jumped" and then settled back into place.

Food and Farming

Farmers in Peru still use terraces, and their methods are very similar to the Incas'. It would be hard to use machines to farm the thin strips of terracing.

Each year Inca **officials** measured the farmland and divided it into *tupus*. These were pieces of land of different sizes that produced a certain amount of food. A couple was given one *tupu* and two llamas when they married. They got more land as they had children—one *tupu* for a boy, and half a *tupu* for a girl.

Much of the land was steep, so the Incas farmed by making **terraces**. This gave them thin bands of flat land to farm. They used bird droppings and human waste to keep the soil fertile. In some places they had to bring water to the fields in stone channels to irrigate (water) the land.

Farmers grew corn and a grain called *quinoa*, which grew well high in the mountains. They also grew potatoes, squash, beans, watermelons, peppers, avocados, pears, plums, and cocoa. They grew cotton and kept llamas and alpacas for their wool. They kept dogs and guinea pigs for meat and hunted wild animals. Food was cooked over an open fire. Ordinary people mostly ate bread, porridge, and vegetables.

Corn was the most important crop. It could be made into flat bread, porridge, and beer. There were religious **ceremonies** when the corn was planted. Everyone, even the *Sapa Inca*, planted corn, but the *Sapa Inca* did not work for long.

This statue shows a shaman. A shaman was part priest, part doctor. They used herbs grown by the farmers in their medicines.

Families

All Incas lived and worked in large family groups called **ayllu**. All the *ayllu* in a village farmed the land together. In all families, no matter how important they were, men and women did different kinds of work. Men worked outside the home. This work could be running the **empire**, making pots in the city, or farming the land. Women worked in the home. Women from ordinary families took care of the children, cooked, and made cloth and baskets. Women from important families made sure that servants did these jobs properly.

The carvings on this bowl show people going about their daily lives. Men farmed and looked after the animals. Women spun wool, wove, and took care of the home and children.

Children were brought up to do the same work as their parents. Girls learned to run a home and make cloth. Boys learned their fathers' jobs. Boys who were going to be government **officials** had to go to special schools to learn how to make and read *quipu*.

Sometimes officials sent ordinary boys who they thought were smart to these schools. They also chose girls to go to schools that trained the *Mamacuna*—the most skilled weavers. Children had to leave their *ayllu* to go to these schools, but it was a way to move into a more important level of Inca life.

This model shows a mother weaving, with her daughter watching.

Clothes

Most people wore hats made from wool or cotton. They were often knitted, but some were woven.

Most Incas wore a similar style of clothing. The cloth was spun and woven from cotton or wool. It was dyed with plant dyes, which made many different colors. Men wore **loincloths** and **tunics**. The length of the tunic varied, depending on the weather. Women wore long tunics with a belt around the middle, or short tunics with a long skirt. Sandals were made from woven leaves and wool or animal skins.

The style of clothes was the same for all Incas. However, you could tell how important a person was by their clothes. Important people wore brightly colored clothing. It was more decorated than clothing worn by ordinary people. It was made well.

All Incas wore capes tied or pinned together over their other clothes.

Homes

Each *ayllu* lived in a set of rooms around a courtyard. People spent most of their time outside. The Incas built their houses from stone or mud bricks on a stone base, with a dirt floor. Roofs were covered in branches, then reeds or grass.

Each room was usually about 13 feet (4 meters) by 5 feet (1.5 meters), with one doorway and no windows. Each room was separate. If a house had two floors, the stairs to the top floor were outside. Ordinary people did not have much furniture, except for a sleeping platform and a few mats. There were places in the wall to store pots and baskets. Clothes were hung on pegs.

Inca homes did not have much furniture, but even ordinary people had decorated pottery bowls and jars.

Homes had very steep roofs, to carry away the rain.

The way this man is dressed shows he is probably the leader of the *ayllu*.

Grinding corn to make bread and porridge took a lot of time.

This woman is using a backstrap loom. She keeps the threads straight by tying them tight behind her back.

End of Empire

In 1525 the Inca **empire** had stopped growing, but it was running smoothly. That year a deadly illness swept the empire. It killed many people, including the *Sapa Inca*. He had just split the empire between two of his sons.

When the Spanish landed at Tumbez in 1532, the Inca empire was split and still weakened by all the deaths from the disease. By 1533 the Spanish had taken over. At first they ruled by using Inca kings who would obey them. But in 1572 they killed the last one of these and put Spanish governors in charge.

The Spanish brought their own beliefs. They did not want the Incas to worship their own gods. In Cuzco they destroyed the Inca **temple** of the Sun god, and built this Catholic church on top of it.

Glossary

ayllu group of related families

ceremony set of acts with religious meaning

duty work work that someone must do for their ruler as a sort of tax

empire group of territories or lands controlled by one country

festival time of celebration

loincloth material that covers the body between the waist and thighs

mortar material used to stick rocks or bricks together

noble important person of high birth

offering something given to a god

official person who runs a country for the ruler

penance something that is done to make up for having done something bad

quipu group of knotted strings used for keeping records

sacrifice kill or destroy something as an offering to a god

spirit being that cannot be seen

temple building for religious worship

terrace flat land made for farming

tunic knee-length belted garment

weft in weaving, one of the threads that runs across the loom

Find Out More

Books

Ganeri, Anita. *The Incas*. Minneapolis: Compass Point, 2006.

Saunders, Nicholas J. *The Inca City of Cuzco*. Milwaukee: World Almanac Library, 2005.

Somervill, Barbara A. *Machu Picchu: City in the Clouds*. New York: Children's Press, 2005.

Websites

www.nationalgeographic.com/ngkids/games/brainteaser/inca/inca.html
Test your knowledge of the Incas with this interactive game.

www.peruvianembassy.us/kids-room-history-inca-empire.php
Learn more about the Inca empire and what happened to it from the Embassy of Peru in Washington, D.C.

Pronunciation Guide

ayllu ay-lee-oo

chasqui CHAS-kee

Chimu CHEE-moo

Cumbi Camayoc KUM-bee ka-MY-ock

curaca koo-rah-kah

Cuzco KOOS-koh

Hatan Runa HAT-an ROO-nah

Inti IN-tee

Machu Picchu MAH-choo PEE-choo

Mamacuna MA-ma KOO-na

mitimaes mit-i-mays

Moche MOH-chay

Quechua KETCH-wah

quinoa KEEN-wah

quipu KEE-poo

Sapa Inca SAH-pah IN-kah

Tahuantinsuyu tah-wan-tin-SOO-you

tupu too-poo

Viracocha weer-ah-KOH-chah

Index